Poptropica English

PUPIL'S BOOK 3

T0386022

Contents

Welcome

1 Look, Sophie! Wow, Oliver! Finley Keen is making a film!

2 Oh, cool! Finley is my favourite film star! Sophie LOVES Finley!

3 Oh, Uncle James, he's funny and clever... Aah...

4 'Can you act? Are you funny, tall and fast? Auditions 1 p.m.' WOW!

5 I'm funnier than you, Sophie. No, you're not.

6 Look! I'm taller than you, Sophie. Hmmm.

2  Listen and read.

Speech bubbles in illustration:

I'm Coco. I've got the script!

And my name's Sophie. I love Finley Keen!

I'm Finley Keen. I'm a film star!

Hello! I'm Uncle James. I like computers. Do you like computers?

Hi! I'm Oliver. I'm ten. I like films.

3 Listen. Say the names.

4 Ask and answer.

Do you like...?   Yes, I do.

No, I don't.

1

Daniel Radcliffe

2

Miranda Cosgrove

3

Zac Efron

4

Robert Pattinson

5

Jennifer Lawrence

5   **Listen and say.** **6**   **Listen and chant.**

morning

afternoon

I get up in the morning,
Have breakfast, go to school.
Home in the afternoon.
That's cool!
Have dinner in the evening,
Then we go and play.
I go to bed at night
And get up the next day...

evening

night

7   **Listen and say.** **8**   **Listen and sing.**

January, February,
March, April,
May or June.
What's your favourite?
What's your favourite?
What's your favourite month?

July, August,
September, October,
November or December.
What's your favourite?
What's your favourite?
What's your favourite month?

9   **Listen and say.** **10**   **Listen and point.**

50 60 70 80 90 100

53 77 54
81 75 89
98 66

1 Free time

1 ⭐ What do you know?

2 🎧 1:14 Listen and find.

skateboarding

playing the guitar

cooking

chatting online

playing computer games

3 🎧 1:15 Listen and tick (✓) or cross (✗).

4 🎧 1:16 Listen and say.

1 ☐

2 ☐

3 ☐

5 ☐

6 ☐

7 ☐

Can identify some free-time activities

watching TV

skiing

5 1:17 **Listen and chant. Count the activities.**

Finley Keen... he's so cool.
He likes playing football,
He likes going to the pool.
Does he like skiing and watching TV?
Yes, he does, just like me!
Does he like singing? Does he like cleaning?
No, he doesn't.
And he doesn't like reading.

 **LOOK!** 1:18

What **does** he/she **like doing**?	He/She **likes skiing**.
Does he/she **like skiing**?	Yes, he/she **does**.
	No, he/she **doesn't**.

6 1:19 **What do Sophie and Oliver like?
Listen, think and choose.**

7 **Ask and answer.**

Does Oliver like cleaning?

No, he doesn't.

Can ask and answer about what people like doing in their free time

8 **Listen and sing.**

What do you, do you like doing?
What do you, do you like doing?

1

Do you like riding your bike?
Yes, I do. I like riding my bike.
Do you like playing the guitar?
Yes, I do. Look! Look! I'm a pop star.

Chorus
Do you like playing computer games?
No, I don't. I like riding my scooter.
Do you like skateboarding, too?
Yes, I like skateboarding! How about you?

Chorus

2

riding my scooter

riding my bike

5

3

4

LOOK! 1:22

What **do** you **like doing**?	
Do you **like playing the guitar**?	Yes, I **do**.
	No, I **don't**.

9 **Look at Activity 8. Ask and answer.**

What do you
like doing?

I like playing
the guitar.

Number 3.

HOME SCHOOL LINK

10 Read and match.

1

2

3

a This is my dog, Timmy. He likes skateboarding. Look! He's cool!

b Hi, I'm Anna. I'm nine. I like singing and playing the guitar with my friends.

c I'm Charlie. I don't like watching TV. I like skiing. My sister doesn't like watching TV, either. She likes skiing with me. It's fun!

11 Listen and answer.

1:23

12 Listen and say.

1:24

SOUNDS FUN!

She likes **sk**iing, **sk**ateboarding and **sk**ipping.

He likes **sw**imming with **sw**ans.

13 Play the game.

Does he like skiing?

Yes, he does.

 15 **Act out the story.**

16 **What do you know?**

17 **1:28 Listen and read. Then tick (✓) and say.**

Do you like my house?

This is Rosa. Look at her house. It's a boat. Rosa likes her boat. She doesn't like watching TV. She likes chatting online and playing the guitar. She also likes riding her bike but not on the boat!

This is Will. This is his house. It's a lighthouse! Will likes living in the lighthouse but he doesn't like climbing the stairs. He likes playing computer games and watching TV. He likes cooking, too.

	Rosa	Will
1 likes chatting online	☐	☐
2 likes cooking	☐	☐
3 likes playing computer games	☐	☐
4 doesn't like climbing the stairs	☐	☐
5 doesn't like watching TV	☐	☐

Rosa likes... Will doesn't like...

PROJECT

Design an unusual house.

1 **Think** about an unusual house.
2 **Draw** a picture of the house.
3 **Write** about things you can do in it.
4 **Share** your design with the class.

Lesson 6 Can understand short texts about what other children like or don't like doing / Can design an unusual house

11

18 **Listen and tick (✓).**

1

a  ☐   b  ☐

2

a  ☐   b  ☐

3

a  ☐   b  ☐

4

a  ☐   b ☐

19 **Write in your notebook.**

1    What does she like doing?
She ❓.

2    ❓?
He likes playing the guitar.

3    Do they like playing computer games?
No, ❓.

4    Does she ❓?
Yes, she does!

20 **Choose a picture. Ask and answer.**

What does he like doing?   He likes cooking.

I can identify some free-time activities.
I can talk about what people like doing in their free time.
I can understand short texts about what other children like doing.

Can assess what I have learnt in Unit 1

21 Write in your notebook.

	Family member 1 (man)	Family member 2 (woman)	Friend 1 (boy)	Friend 2 (girl)
Me				
My friend				

22 Now play.

Friend 1. Does he like skateboarding?

No, he doesn't.

Does he like cooking?

No, he doesn't.

Does he like watching TV?

No, he doesn't. My turn.

Now go to Poptropica English World

Wider World 1

At the weekend

1 ⭐ What do you know?

2 🎧 1:31 Listen and read. Who has got a brother?

> Hi, I'm Kelly. I'm from Canada. It's snowy here. I like skiing. It's fun. I can go very fast. Do you like skiing?

> Hi, I'm Tumelo. I'm from South Africa. I like playing football at school with my friends. I can see the Soccer City stadium from my house. It's really big. My favourite team is the Mamelodi Sundowns.

3 🎧 1:32 Listen and say the names.

Can understand texts about what other children like doing at the weekend

3

Hi, I'm Anne. I'm from France. I like riding my bike with my mum and dad. It's good exercise. I like riding my bike on sunny days. My little brother likes riding, too!

4

Hi, I'm Carlos. I'm from Mexico. Look! I'm at a beautiful water park in Cancun. I like swimming and going down the stream with my friends. It's great!

4 **Read, think and tick (✓) or cross (✗).**

1 Kelly can't ski fast.

2 Tumelo likes playing football at school.

3 Anne likes riding her bike with her family.

4 Carlos goes to the water park with his family.

5  **Ask your friend about his/her hobbies.**

Do you like playing football?   Yes, I do.

Tell the class

2 Animals

1 ⭐ **What do you know?**

2 🎧 1:33 **Listen and find.**

lion

elephant

meat

crocodile

giraffe

grass

3 🎧 1:34 **Listen and tick (✓) or cross (✗).**

4 🎧 1:35 **Listen and say.**

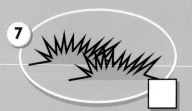

Can identify some animals and their food

monkey

hippo

fruit

leaves

4

8

5 1:37 **Listen and chant. Circle the animals.**

Do hippos eat insects?
No, they don't. Hippos eat grass.

Do monkeys eat grass?
No, they don't. Monkeys eat fruit.

Do lions eat meat?
Yes, they do. Lions eat meat.

Do giraffes eat leaves?
Yes, they do. Giraffes eat leaves.

LOOK! 1:38

What **do** giraffes **eat**? They **eat** leaves.		
Do giraffes **eat**	leaves?	**Yes**, they **do**.
	meat?	**No**, they **don't**.

6 1:39 **Listen and say the missing words.**

1 Crocodiles eat ❓ , too.

2 Giraffes eat ❓ !

3 Do hippos eat ❓ ?

4 They eat fruit. They ❓ fruit!

7 **Ask and answer.**

What do giraffes eat?

They eat leaves.

8 1:40 / 1:41 **Listen and sing.**

 SONG

Lions live in Africa.
They're big and strong.
They like sleeping all day long.
They run very fast
To catch their lunch.
What do they eat?
They eat meat.
Crunch, crunch, munch!

Oscar lives with me.
He's a very small cat.
He likes sleeping in my flat.
He runs very fast
To get his lunch.
What does he eat?
He eats meat.
Crunch, crunch, munch!

sleeping

1:42 **LOOK!**

Lions **live** in Africa.
They **live** in Africa.
My cat **lives** with me.
He/She/It **lives** with me.

9 **Look at Activity 8. Ask and answer.**

HOME SCHOOL LINK

They eat meat.

He eats meat.

Lions.

Oscar.

18 **Lesson 3**   Can talk about where animals live and what they eat

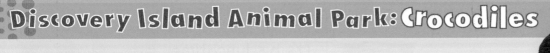

10 Look and read. What do crocodiles eat?

Discovery Island Animal Park: Crocodiles

Hi, I'm Paul. There are a lot of crocodiles here at the Animal Park. This is Snapper. Look at the bird in her mouth! It's cleaning her teeth.

These crocodiles live in rivers in Africa and Australia. They are very big and strong. They like sleeping in the sun and swimming. Crocodiles eat meat and fish. They can eat you too, so watch out!

11 🎧 1:44 Listen and answer.

12 🎧 1:45 Listen and say.

SOUNDS FUN!

Sixteen green leaves are a treat to eat.

Thirteen lions like eating meat and sleeping.

13 Play the game.

Snap! They're crocodiles.

Crocodiles eat meat.

14 1:48 **Talk about the pictures. Then listen and read.**

STORY

15 **Act out the story.**

16 What do you know?

17 Listen and read. Then tick (✓) or cross (✗).

Amazing Animals!

Elephants

Elephants live in Africa and India. They don't eat meat. They have only got four teeth. They eat a lot of grass, leaves, fruit and flowers. Elephants can say hello with their trunks.

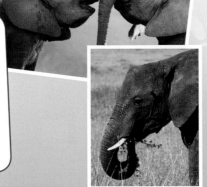

Giraffes

Giraffes live in Africa. They're taller than elephants. They eat leaves from tall trees. They also eat fruit and flowers. They don't drink every day. They can live for one week with no water. They have got long black tongues. They can clean their ears with their tongues!

1 Elephants eat a lot. ☐

2 Elephants have got a lot of teeth. ☐

3 Elephants say hello with their ears. ☐

4 Giraffes drink a lot of water. ☐

5 Giraffes have got pink tongues. ☐

6 Giraffes are taller than elephants. ☐

PROJECT

Write about an amazing animal.

1 **Think** about an amazing animal.
2 **Draw** or print a picture of the animal.
3 **Write** five interesting facts about the animal.
4 **Share** your facts with the class.

18 Listen and tick (✓).

1

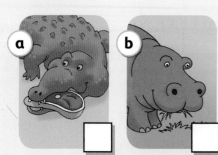

a   b

2

a   b

3

a   b

4

a   b

19 Write in your notebook.

1 Do lions eat meat?
Yes, ? .

2 What do giraffes eat?
They ? .

3 Do crocodiles eat fruit?
No, ? .

4 What do birds eat?
They ? .

20 Choose a picture from Activity 18. Ask and answer.

Where do giraffes live?

They live in Africa.

 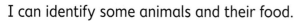

I can identify some animals and their food.
I can talk about animals.
I can understand short texts about animals.

Do they live in the forests?

No, they don't.

Do they eat fish?

Yes, they do.

Do they live in rivers?

Yes, they do.

Now go to Poptropica English World

1 ⭐ What do you know?

2 🎧 1:51 Listen and find.

STORM-MACHINE

RAINMAKER MKIII

SNOWMAKER MK.IV

storm

KA-BOOM!

the sun

cloud

hot

rain

wet

snow

cold

3 🎧 1:52 Listen and tick (✓) or cross (✗).

4 🎧 1:53 Listen and say.

1 2 3 4 5

Can identify some weather words

wind

5 1:54 **Listen and chant. Circle the weather words.**

What's the weather like today?
It's cloudy and rainy. We're sad, we can't play.

What's the weather like today?
It's snowy and windy. We're sad, we can't play.
What's the weather like today?
It's cold, wet and stormy. We're scared,
we can't play.

What's the weather like today?
It's hot and sunny. We're happy, let's play!

1:55 **LOOK!**

| What's the weather like today? | It's rainy and wet. |

6 1:56 **Listen and number.**

a ☐   b ☐   c ☐

d ☐   e ☐

6 ☐

7 **Ask and answer.**

What's the weather like today?   It's...

8 **Listen and sing.**

 **SONG**

 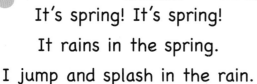

Spring, summer, autumn, winter.
Four seasons in a year.

It's spring! It's spring!
It rains in the spring.
I jump and splash in the rain.
Chorus
It's summer! It's summer!
The sun shines in the summer.
I splash and swim in the sea.
Chorus

It's autumn! It's autumn!
The wind blows in the autumn.
I fly my kite in the sky.
Chorus
It's winter! It's winter!
It snows in the winter.
I laugh and play in the snow.

spring

splash

summer

autumn

kite

winter

 1:60 **LOOK!**

It rain**s** in the spring.
I splash in the rain.

9 **Look at Activity 8. Ask and answer.**

It snows. I play
in the snow.

It's winter.

HOME
SCHOOL
LINK

Can identify activities you can do in different seasons

10 **Read and match.**

1 **2** My favourite season **3** **4**

spring   summer   autumn   winter

a It's windy and I can fly my kite. There are a lot of apples on the tree in my garden. Yum!

b It's hot and there's no school! I go to the park and I eat a lot of fruit. My favourites are strawberries and peaches. What's your favourite season?

c I like flowers. The birds sing in the trees. I like listening to the rain.

d It snows and it's lovely. Some birds don't like the cold and they fly to hot places. Some animals sleep.

11 1:61 **Listen and name the season.**

SOUNDS FUN!

12 1:62 **Listen and say.**

The wind bl**ow**s the sn**ow** on the rainb**ow**. There's a m**ou**se in a h**ou**se in the cl**ou**ds.

13 **Play the game.**

Rain!

 STORY

16 **What do you know?**

17 **1:66 Listen and read. Then tick (✓) or cross (✗).**

HURRICANE

Do you like storms?
This man likes storms. He's flying into a hurricane with his camera.

What is a hurricane?
A hurricane is a big storm. There's a lot of wind and rain. The hurricane goes around in a big circle. It can knock down trees and houses. There are big waves on the sea, too.

What's the eye of a hurricane?
The eye is the centre of the hurricane. It isn't windy and rainy there. Can you see the eye of the hurricane in the photo?

When are there hurricanes?
There are hurricanes in the summer and the autumn.

1 The man with the camera likes storms. ☐

2 A hurricane is a big storm. ☐

3 It's hot and sunny in a hurricane. ☐

4 The eye isn't the centre of the hurricane. ☐

18 **Cover Activity 17. Ask and answer.**

1 What is a hurricane?

2 What's the eye of a hurricane?

3 When are there hurricanes?

 **PROJECT**

Make a mini-book about a natural disaster.

1 **Think** about a natural disaster.
2 **Fold** a piece of paper to make a mini-book. Draw or stick photos in your book.
3 **Write** about the natural disaster in your book.
4 **Share** your ideas with the class.

19   1:68 **Listen and tick (✓).**

1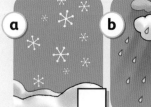

2

3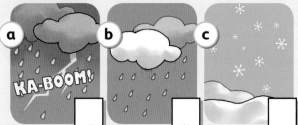

4

20 **Write in your notebook.**

1  I like swimming in the ❔ .

2  I like riding my bike ❔ .

3  I like walking ❔ .

4  I like skiing ❔ .

21   **Choose a picture. Ask and answer.**

Picture 1b. What's the weather like?

It's wet.

I can identify some weather words.

I can talk about the seasons and activities.

I can understand a text about hurricanes.

22 Draw the chart in your notebook.
Then write.

	Spring	Summer	Autumn	Winter
Me				
My friend	☐	☐	☐	☐

23 Now play.

Summer. You like swimming.

No, my turn.

**Now go to Poptropica
English World**

Wider World 2

Wildlife parks

1 **What do you know?**

2 **Listen and read.**
1:69
Which animals eat leaves?

I'm Surian. I live in Borneo. There is an orangutan centre near my house. Baby orangutans are cute. They drink milk and eat bananas every day. Orangutans have got long red hair and long arms. They live in the rainforests. They like climbing trees.

I'm James. I live in London. I like going to the zoo to see animals. My favourite animals are the lions. There are some cute lion cubs, too. They like playing but they've got sharp claws.

3 **Read and say the names.**

1 He lives in London.

2 They drink milk and eat bananas.

3 They eat the leaves at the top of the trees.

4 They've got sharp claws.

5 His house is near an orangutan centre.

Can understand texts about wildlife parks

3 I'm Akeyo. I live in the Serengeti National Park in Kenya. The sun shines every day here and it's very hot. There are a lot of different animals in the park. I like the giraffes. They're tall and they've got long necks. They eat the leaves off the tops of the trees.

 4 **Read and answer in your notebook.**

1 Where do orangutans live?

2 What do baby orangutans eat?

3 What does James like doing?

4 Where does Akeyo live?

5 Which animals does Akeyo like?

 5 **Ask and answer.**

1 Is there a zoo near you? Which animals can you see there?

2 Do you go to the zoo with your family?

3 Are there national parks in your country? Where are they?

4 What's your favourite animal? Does it live in your country?

Tell the Class

4 My week

study English

Hello!

1 What do you know?

2 **2:01** Listen and find.

practise the piano

study maths

$10 \times 0.5 =$

have music lessons

have ballet lessons

learn to draw

3 **2:02** Listen and tick (✓) or cross (✗).

4 **2:03** Listen and say.

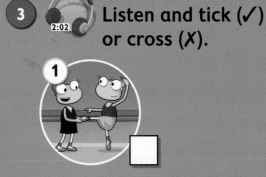

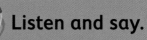

Can identify some scheduled activities

5 🎧 2:04 **Listen and chant. Point to the clocks.**

do gymnastics

do karate

What do you do on Saturdays?
What do you do on Saturdays?
I do gymnastics at 10 o'clock.
She does gymnastics at 10 o'clock.
I go swimming at 11 o'clock.
He goes swimming at 11 o'clock.
I have ballet lessons at half past 2.
She has ballet lessons at half past 2.
I go skateboarding at 4 o'clock.
He goes skateboarding at 4 o'clock.

🎧 2:05 **LOOK!**

I **go** swimming at 11 o'clock.
He **goes** swimming at 11 o'clock.

6 🎧 2:06 **Listen and read. Then tick (✓) or cross (✗).**

1 Oliver studies Maths at 9 o'clock. ☐

2 Sophie studies English at half past 3. ☐

3 Phil O'Fax does gymnastics at 4 o'clock. ☐

4 Finley Keen practises the piano at half past 8. ☐

7 **Ask and answer.**

What do you do on Saturdays?

I do karate on Saturdays.

8 2:08 / 2:09 **Listen and sing.**

How does she go to school?

Does she go by bike or car?

Does she go by bus or does she walk?
Is it very far? Is it very far?

She goes to school by bus.
Yes, she goes to school by bus.

She doesn't go by bike or car.

She goes to school by bus.

How does he go to the park?

Does he go by bike or car?

Does he go by bus or does he walk?
Is it very far? Is it very far?

He goes to the park by bike.
Yes, he goes to the park by bike.

He doesn't walk or go by bus.

He goes to the park by bike.

2:10 **LOOK!**

How **does** she **go** to school?

She **goes** to school **by bus**.

He **walks** to the park.

HOME SCHOOL LINK

9 **Play the game.**

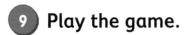

How does he go to school?

Two. He goes to school by bike.

10 **Look and read. What does Fifi do at 2 o'clock?**

What does Fifi do on Saturdays?

She has a busy day!
She has ballet lessons
in the morning.
She loves dancing!

How does she go to her ballet lesson? Does she walk?

No, she goes by car!
She doesn't like
walking.

What time does she have her ballet lesson?

At 10 o'clock.

What does she do in the afternoon?

She goes skateboarding
in the park at 2 o'clock.
Then she goes to a party
with her friends. She has a
lot of fun on Saturdays!

11 **Listen and answer.** *True* or *false*?

12 **Listen and say.**

SOUNDS FUN!

She goes swimming
and has music lessons.
Does she?
Yes, she does.

13 **Play the game.**

What do you do
on Saturdays?

You do
karate.

Talk about the pictures. Then listen and read.

  Act out the story.

Can understand a simple story / Can act out a story

16 **What do you know?**

17 **Listen and read. Then match.**

How do you go to school?

1 Lanau doesn't go to school by car. His family hasn't got a car. There aren't many roads where he lives but there are a lot of rivers. So Lanau and his friends go to school by boat. Their school is on the water, too!

2 Ricky doesn't go to school! His school is very far away. He has classes at home – on the internet. On Fridays, his teacher goes to his house by plane.

3 Susanna lives in a cold place. She doesn't walk to school. She goes to school by skidoo. She likes riding her skidoo. It's cool!

a

b

c

18 **Find the words.**

cold   boat   home

skidoo   teacher   car

**PROJECT**

How does your class go to school? Do a survey.

1 **Ask** your classmates: How do you go to school?
2 **Write** down the answers.
3 **Draw** and colour a diagram to show the results.
4 **Share** the results with the class.

19 **Look at Activity 17. Ask and answer.**

Does Susanna go to school by boat?

No, she doesn't.

20 **Listen and tick (✓).**

1

2

3

4

21 **Write in your notebook.**

1  What does she do on Mondays?

2  She ? on Mondays and Wednesdays.

3   ? ?

She studies English on Saturdays and Sundays.

4   When ? ?

He does karate at half past 2 on Sundays.

22 **Choose a picture. Ask and answer.**

What does he do on Thursdays?   He studies English.

I can identify some scheduled activities.
I can talk about scheduled activities.
I can understand short texts about how other children go to school.

23 Draw the chart in your notebook. Then write.

	Me	**My friend**	
Monday			☐
Tuesday			☐
Wednesday			☐
Thursday			☐
Friday			☐
Saturday			☐
Sunday			☐

24 Now play.

You practise the piano on Mondays.

Yes! My turn.

Now go to Poptropica English World

5 Jobs

a film star

1 What do you know?

2 2:20 Listen and find.

a basketball player

a mechanic

a police officer

an astronaut

a firefighter

a builder

a ballet dancer

3 2:21 Listen and tick (✓) or cross (✗).

4 2:22 Listen and say.

1 2 3 4

6 7 8

Can identify some common jobs

a photographer

5 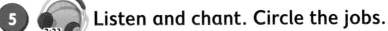 2:23 **Listen and chant. Circle the jobs.**

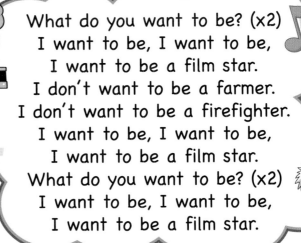

What do you want to be? (x2)
I want to be, I want to be,
I want to be a film star.
I don't want to be a farmer.
I don't want to be a firefighter.
I want to be, I want to be,
I want to be a film star.
What do you want to be? (x2)
I want to be, I want to be,
I want to be a film star.

2:24 **LOOK!**

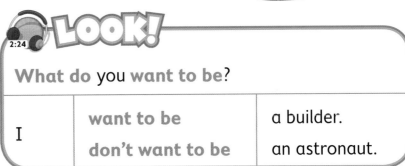

What do you want to be?

I	want to be	a builder.
	don't want to be	an astronaut.

6  2:25 **Read and match. Then listen and check.**

1 I want to be a ballet dancer.

2 I want to be a farmer.

3 I want to be a basketball player.

4 I want to be a police officer.

Al   Ben   Cathy   Di

7  **Ask and answer.**

What do you want to be?   I want to be a police officer.

8   **Listen and sing.**

2:27 / 2:28

> Teacher, farmer, builder, doctor,
> What does he want to be?
> Teacher, farmer, builder, doctor,
> Just a minute! Let me see...

Does he want to be a teacher?
No, no, no, he doesn't.

Does he want to be a farmer?
No, no, no, he doesn't.

Does he want to be a builder?
No, no, no, he doesn't.

Does he want to be a doctor?
Yes, yes, yes, he does.

He wants to be a doctor.

Chorus

builder   teacher

doctor   farmer

LOOK!

2:29

Does he/she want to be a builder?	Yes, he/she does.
	No, he/she doesn't.

9 **Play the game.**

Does she want to be a teacher?

Yes, she does.

Number 2.

1	X	X	✓	X
2	X	X	X	✓
3	X	✓	X	X
4	✓	X	X	X

10 **Read and match.**

1

2

3

4

 Mary

 Emma

 Tim

 Bob

I like dancing. I have ballet lessons on Saturdays. I want to be a ballet dancer.

I can sing and dance. I can act, too. I don't want to be a ballet dancer. I want to be a film star.

I'm strong. I like climbing. I like helping people. I don't want to be a police officer. I want to be a firefighter.

I like running. I can jump and I can catch a ball. I'm very tall. I want to be a basketball player.

11  **Look at Activity 10. Listen and answer.**

12 **Listen and say.**

SOUNDS FUN!

The farm**er** and the firefight**er** like past**a**.
The doct**or** and the build**er** like pizz**a**.

13 **Play the game.**

I want to be a firefighter.

15   **Act out the story.**

16 **What do you know?**

17 2:36 **Listen, read and match.**

I WANT TO BE A CHAMPION!

1 Naomi Johnson wants to be a champion. She wants to win three medals at the next Olympic Games. She wants to be the best!

2 At 6 o'clock in the morning Naomi goes swimming. She swims for two hours. Then she has a big breakfast. She eats four eggs, a lot of bread, cheese and fruit. Then she goes running. At 12 o'clock, she has chicken and pasta for lunch. In the afternoon, she goes swimming again. She swims 70–80 km every week!

3 Sundays are a special day. Naomi doesn't go swimming. She likes watching TV and she goes shopping. She loves shoes!

a

b

c

18   **Ask and answer.**

1 What/want to be?

2 What time/play/go/do...?

3 What/eat for breakfast?

4 What/do after lunch?

5 What/do on Sundays?

> What do you want to be?

> I want to be a tennis champion.

Make a collage about your dream job.

1 **Think** about what you want to be.
2 **Make** a collage about your dream job.
3 **Talk** about your dream job with a classmate.
4 **Share** your ideas with the class.

19 **Listen and tick (✓).**

1
 **a**   **b**

2
a    **b**

3
a    **b**

4
a    **b**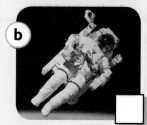

20 **Write in your notebook.**

1

Does he want to be a photographer?

Yes, **?** .

2

Does **?** ?

No, she doesn't.

3 What does he want to be? He **?** mechanic.

4 What **?** ? I want to be a firefighter.

21 **Choose a picture. Ask and answer.**

What does he want to be?

He wants to be a builder.

I CAN

I can identify some common jobs.

I can ask and answer about what people want to be.

I can understand short texts about what other children want to be.

Can assess what I have learnt in Unit 5

22 Choose and draw in your notebook. Then write. **HAVE FUN**

astronaut   ballet dancer   basketball player   builder

doctor   firefighter   mechanic   photographer   police officer

Round 1

My dream job

I want to be _____
_____ .

Round 2

_____'s dream job

(name of brother, sister or friend)

_____ wants to be _____

_____ .

23 Now play.

Round 1

Do you want to be a firefighter?   No, I don't.

Round 2

Does he/she want to be a teacher?   Yes, he/she does! Well done!

Now go to Poptropica English World

Wider World 3

My hero

1 **What do you know?**

2 **Listen and read. Does Kate want to be a photographer?**

Hi! I'm Alejandro. I'm from Spain and I love basketball. I play every week. I want to be a famous basketball player. My favourite basketball player is Pau Gasol. He's from Spain but he plays in the United States.

My name is Elena. I'm from Russia and I want to be a ballet dancer. I go to ballet school and I have ballet lessons every day. My favourite ballet dancer is Natalia Osipova. She's from Russia.

3  **Read and say the names.**

Who wants to be...

1	a ballet dancer?	2	a film star?
3	a basketball player?	4	a football player?

Can understand short texts about other children's heroes

3 I'm Santiago. I'm from Argentina. I want to be a football player. My favourite team is Boca Juniors. My favourite football player is Lionel Messi. He scores a lot of goals.

4 Hello! I'm Kate. I'm from Ireland. I have singing and dancing lessons at school. I want to be a film star. My favourite film star is Emma Watson.

4 **Read and tick (✓) or cross (✗).**

1   Alejandro plays basketball every day.   ☐

2   Pau Gasol is from the United States.   ☐

3   Elena has ballet lessons every day.   ☐

4   Santiago hasn't got a favourite football team.   ☐

5   Kate doesn't like film stars.   ☐

5  **Work with a friend. Talk about a famous person you admire.**

1   What's his/her name?

2   What does he/she do?

3   Where is he/she from?

4   What can he/she do?

Tell the Class

6 Rainforest

1 ⭐ **What do you know?**

2 🎧 2:41 **Listen and find.**

valley

path

bridge

river

3 🎧 2:42 **Listen and tick (✓) or cross (✗).**

4 🎧 2:43 **Listen and say.**

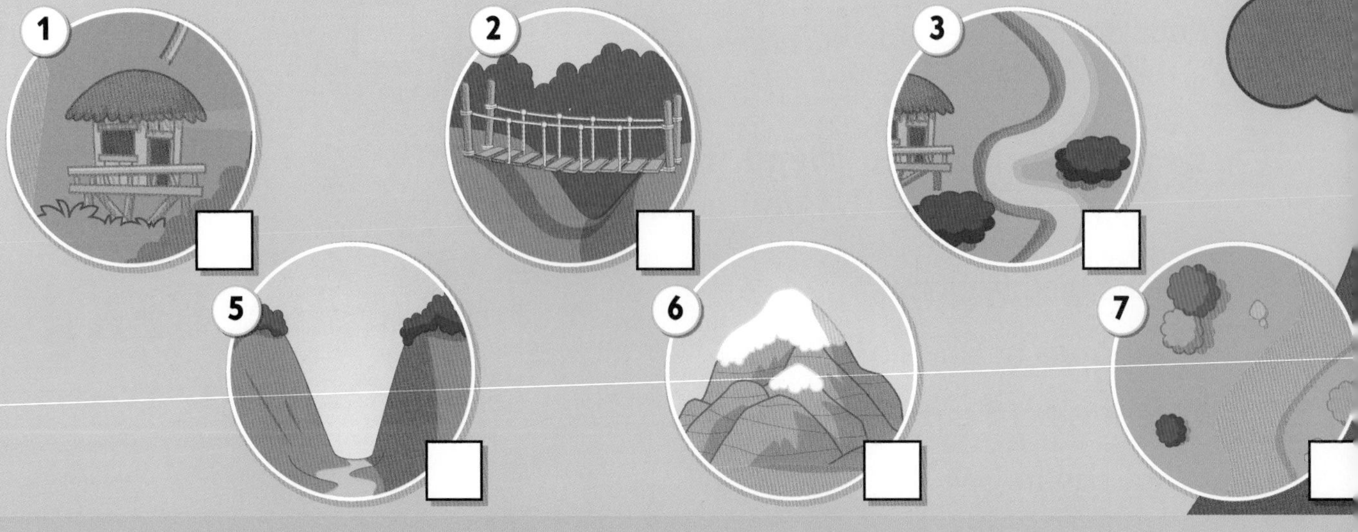

1
2
3
5
6
7

Can identify some places in the rainforest

mountain

hut

cave

waterfall

5 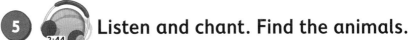 2:44 **Listen and chant. Find the animals.**

Where's the fish?
It's under the bridge.
Where's the snake?
It's behind the tree.
Where's the bird?
It's next to the mountain.
Where's the frog?
It's in front of the tree.

2:45 **LOOK!**

Where's the snake?	It's	behind the mountain.
		next to the waterfall.
Where are the crocodiles?	They're	under the bridge.
		in front of the hut.

6 2:46 **Where are they? Listen and say the missing words.**

1 Sophie is ❓ Uncle James.

2 Coco is ❓ the cave.

3 The hut is ❓ the waterfall.

4 The crocodiles are ❓ the bridge.

7 **Ask and answer.**

Where's Oliver?

He's next to the bridge.

8

8 **Listen and sing.**

Animals live all around us,
All around you and me.
Animals live in the forest,
The mountains and the sea.

Monkeys live in the forest
And they can swing in the trees.
They've got long arms and curly tails
And they can swing in the trees.
Chorus
Eagles live in the mountains
And they can fly in the sky.
They've got sharp claws and silent wings
And they can fly in the sky.
Chorus
Whales live in the sea
And they can swim and sing.
They've got strong tails and tiny eyes
And they can swim and sing.
Chorus

sharp claws

silent wings

curly tails

strong tails

tiny eyes

LOOK!

2:49

They've got	curly/strong tails.
	silent wings.
	tiny eyes.
	sharp claws.

9 **Look at Activity 8. Ask and answer.**

They've got curly tails.

Monkeys.

 HOME SCHOOL LINK

Can talk about where animals live and what they can do

10 **Look and read. Which animals live near the Victoria Falls?**

Victoria Falls

Today I'm at Victoria Falls. There are a lot of big waterfalls here. They are on the Zambezi River. You can go by boat on the river and watch the animals.

 It's cool! There are elephants, giraffes, monkeys, crocodiles and hippos.

Hippo is short for hippopotamus. Do you know that 'hippopotamus' means 'river horse'?

Look! You can see a hippo in the river. Hippos are very big and strong. They've got big jaws with a lot of big, sharp teeth. They've got short legs and big feet.

They can swim. They move their feet on the river bed like ballet dancers and walk in the water!

11 2:51 **Listen and answer. *True* or *false*?**

12 2:52 **Listen and say.**

SOUNDS FUN!

Walk in the mountains and listen to the autumn trees.

13 **Play the game.**

The eagle is next to the rainforest.

Lesson 4 — Can read and talk about the environment / Can pronounce words that include silent letters — 55

Talk about the pictures. Then listen and read.

15 **Act out the story.**

Can understand a simple story / Can act out a story

6

16 What do you know?

17 Listen and read. Then tick (✓) or cross (✗).

2:56

The Amazon Rainforest

It's hot and wet in the Amazon rainforest and there are a lot of tall trees. The Amazon River runs through the rainforest. It's very long. A lot of animals live in the rainforest and the river.

hummingbird

These birds are very small. They drink nectar from flowers. They like red, orange and yellow flowers.

tapir

These animals have got short necks. They live next to the river. They eat leaves and fruit. They love bananas.

These big spiders have got long legs. They live under the leaves on the ground. They can eat a bird or a mouse.

giant tarantula

1   It's hot and wet in the Amazon. ☐

2   Hummingbirds like blue flowers. ☐

3   Tapirs eat meat. ☐

4   Giant tarantulas live in trees. ☐

18 Describe one of the animals in Activity 17. Ask your friend to guess.

Make a fact file about a rainforest animal.

1 **Choose** a rainforest animal.
2 **Draw** a picture or find a photo of the animal.
3 **Write** some facts about your animal.
4 **Share** the facts with the class.

19 2:57 **Listen and tick (✓).**

1  a    b   2  a    b

3  a    b   4  a    b

20 **Write in your notebook.**

1   Where's the giraffe?
It's ❓ the hut.

2   Where are the hippos?
They're ❓ the bridge.

3   Where's the elephant?
It's ❓ .

4   Where are the eagles?
They're ❓ .

21 **Look at Activity 19. Choose a picture.
Then ask and answer.**

Picture 4a. Where's the lion?   It's in the cave.

 **I CAN**

I can identify some places in the rainforest.
I can talk about where things are.
I can understand a text about the rainforest.

22 Spot the differences. Ask and answer.

a   b

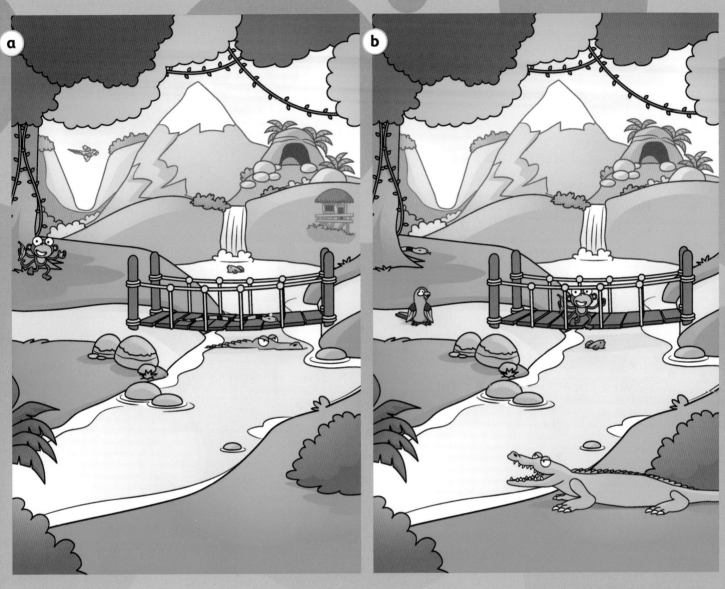

Where's the snake in your picture?

It's on the bridge.

Your turn.

Where's the monkey in your picture?

Now go to Poptropica
English World

Lesson 8

Can use what I have learnt in Unit 6

7 Feelings

1 ⭐ **What do you know?**

2 🎧 3:01 **Listen and find.**

WILD WEST STUDIOS

happy

sad

angry

scared

3 🎧 3:02 **Listen and circle.**

4 🎧 3:03 **Listen and say.**

1 sad / angry

2 scared / hungry

3 tired / sad

5 happy / tired

6 tired / thirsty

Can identify some feelings

tired

DINO PARK

happy / angry

sad / scared

5 **Listen and chant. Circle the feelings.**

1 smiling

Why is she smiling?
Because she's happy.
Why is she crying?
Because she's sad.
Why is he drinking?
Because he's thirsty.
Why is he eating?
Because he's hungry.
Why is he shouting?
Because he's angry.
Why is she laughing?
Because it's funny!

2 crying

3 shouting

4 laughing

 **LOOK!**

| **Why** is he/she laughing? | He's/She's laughing **because** it's funny. |

6 **Listen and answer. *True* or *false*?**

1 Sophie is smiling.

2 Oliver is shouting.

3 Finley Keen is crying.

4 Coco is laughing.

7 **Ask and answer.**

Number 1. Why is she smiling?

Because she's happy.

8 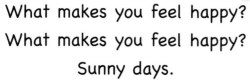 **Listen and sing.**

What makes you feel happy?
What makes you feel happy?
Sunny days.
Sunny days and holidays
Make me feel happy.

What makes you cry?
What makes you cry?
Sad films.
Sad films and long goodbyes
Make me cry.

What makes you feel scared?
What makes you feel scared?
Big storms.
Big storms and green monsters
Make me feel scared.

What makes you laugh?
What makes you laugh?
My friends.
My friends and naughty monkeys
Make me laugh.

naughty

9 **Look at Activity 8. Ask and answer.**

cry   feel angry   feel happy
feel sad   feel scared   laugh

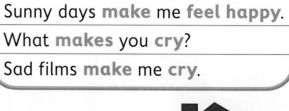
LOOK!
What **makes** you **feel happy**?
Sunny days **make** me **feel happy**.
What **makes** you **cry**?
Sad films **make** me **cry**.

What makes you feel scared?   Storms make me feel scared.

Can talk about how you feel and what makes you feel that way

10 **Look and read. What does Ricky do with his friends?**

RICKY FANTASTIC

Dear Ricky
What makes you feel happy?
Sam

Hi Sam,
Singing and playing the guitar make me feel happy. My friends make me feel happy because they make me laugh. We go skateboarding and play computer games. What makes you laugh?
Ricky

Funny films make me laugh. My brother makes me laugh because he can make funny faces. But it makes me feel sad when he doesn't want to play football with me. What makes you feel sad?
Sam

Winter makes me feel sad because it's cold. But I love summer. Sunny days make me feel happy.
Ricky

11 **Listen and answer.**

12 **Listen and say.**

SOUNDS FUN!

Harry

Henry

Harry's angry and Henry's **h**ungry. Henry's **h**ungry and **H**arry's angry.

13 **Play the game.**

Snap!

I'm hungry.

1 Ooh! The Dinosaur Park Studio!

DINO PARK

Dinosaurs make me feel scared...

2 What's the matter, Oliver?

STOMP! STOMP!

I'm a bit worried!

3 What's that noise?

ROAR!

I'm very scared. Can we go now?

4 Ahhgh!

A dinosaur! Quick! Run!

5 Don't worry! It's not a real dinosaur.

Phew! I'm happy now.

6 It's Coco! Look, he's laughing.

ROAR! Ha ha!

15 **Act out the story.**

Can understand a simple story / Can act out a story

16 What do you know?

17 Listen to the music.
How does it make you feel?

18 Listen and read. Then number.

1 Funny boys

2 MONSTER 3

3 THE SAD GOODBYE

4 Dancing Toes

a It's the end of the film. They're at the train station. They're friends and they're saying goodbye. They're crying. It makes me feel sad. It makes me cry, too.

b There are a lot of people. They're laughing. They're learning to dance. The music is great. It makes me feel happy. I want to sing and dance, too.

c There are two boys. They have a lot of fun. They're funny. They make me laugh.

d There's a big, green monster. The monster has got big, sharp teeth. It makes me feel scared.

19  Look at Activity 18.
Ask and answer.

How does number 3 make you feel?

It makes me feel sad.

PROJECT

Make a feelings box.

1 **Find** a shoe box and decorate it.
2 **Collect** things that make you feel happy, sad, scared...
3 **Write** about your feelings. Stick notes on the things.
4 **Share** your feelings box with your class.

20  Listen and tick (✓).

21 Write in your notebook.

1  Why 🔢 ?

Because he's angry.

2   Why are you 🔢 ?

Because it's 11 o'clock.

3  Why are you smiling?

🔢 it's my birthday.

4 What 🔢 feel happy?

Going to the beach makes me feel happy.

22  Choose a picture. Ask and answer.

Why is she crying? Because she's saying 'goodbye'.

I CAN

I can identify some feelings.

I can talk about feelings using *Why* and *because*.

I can recognise how music and films make me feel.

66 Lesson 7

Can assess what I have learnt in Unit 7

23 Read and match.

I'm smiling because it's Friday.

I'm sad because it's rainy.

I'm tired because it's Monday.

I'm hungry because it's lunch time.

I'm angry because it's noisy.

I'm happy because it's the holidays.

I'm scared because there's a spider.

24 Now play.

Are you crying?

Yes.

Why are you crying?

Because my mum is angry.

Now go to Poptropica
English World

Wider World 4

It makes me feel happy

1 ⭐ **What do you know?**

2 🎧 3:19 **Listen and read. Where are the children from?**

dragon dance

1
lantern

I'm Zhi. I'm from China. Lunar New Year makes me feel happy because it's fun. It's in January or February and it's called the Spring Festival. There are dragons and pretty lanterns. We visit family and friends.

I'm Diego. I'm from Peru. Dancing makes me feel happy because it's good exercise. Here I am with my friends. We're dancing and wearing traditional dress and hats. Do you like our clothes?

2
traditional dress

fireworks
3

My name's Mark. I'm from the United Kingdom. Bonfire Night makes me feel happy because it's fun. It's in November. I go to watch fireworks in the park with my family. I'm not scared of fireworks. In the photo, we're wearing hats and scarves because it's cold.

Can understand texts about what makes people happy

4

Hi! I'm Victoria. I sing in the African Children's Choir. At school we have singing and dancing lessons every day. We go by bus and train to other schools and sing in concerts. Singing in the choir makes me feel happy because I love music.

choir

3 3:20 **Listen and say the names.**

4 **Read and answer in your notebook.**

1   When is Lunar New Year?

2   Why does dancing make Diego feel happy?

3   Is Mark scared of fireworks?

4   How does Victoria's choir go to other schools?

5 **Ask and answer.**

1   What activity or festival makes you feel happy?

2   When is it?

3   What do you do?

4   What do you wear?

5   Why does it make you feel happy?

Tell the Class

8 By the sea

1 ⭐ **What do you know?**

2 🎧 3:21 **Listen and find.**

surfing

sailing

fishing

sea

snorkelling

beach

3 🎧 3:22 **Listen and tick (✓) or cross (✗).**

4 🎧 3:23 **Listen and say.**

1

2

3

5

6

Can identify some outdoor activities

5   **Listen and chant. How does the shark feel?**

3:24

What are you scared of?
I'm scared of sharks.
What are you scared of?
I'm scared of sharks.

I like the beach and I like the sea.
But I'm scared of sharks
And they're scared of me!

kayaking

horse-riding

 **LOOK!**

3:25

| What are you **scared of**? | I'm **scared of** sharks. |

6  **Listen and answer the questions.**

3:26

1   What are you scared of, Sophie?

2   What are you scared of, Finley Keen?

3   What are you scared of, Oliver?

7 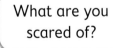 **Ask six friends.**

4

What are you
scared of?

I'm scared of
insects.

8 **Listen and sing.**

What am I keen on?
I'm keen on these:
Film stars and fishing,
Pasta and cheese.

What am I bored with?
I'm bored with these:
Dancing and toy cars,
Watching TV.

What am I scared of?
I'm scared of these:
Lions and crocodiles
Spiders and bees.
Anything else, you ask?
I'm terrified of sharks!

bee

LOOK! 3:29

I'm **scared of** lions.
I'm **bored with** watching TV.
I'm **keen on** fishing.
I'm **terrified of** sharks.

HOME SCHOOL LINK

 **9** **Look at Activity 8. Ask and answer.**

cooking   crocodiles   football
horse-riding   spiders
surfing   swimming

bored with   keen on
scared of   terrified of

Football.

I'm bored with football.

Can say how I feel about hobbies and animals

10 **Look and read. What is Tom scared of?**

Dear Granny and Grandad,

I'm having fun here on holiday. It's hot and sunny and there are a lot of things to do. I like swimming in the sea. The sea is beautiful and blue. There aren't any sharks but there are dolphins. I'm not scared of dolphins. They eat fish. They don't eat people. I like swimming with them. It makes me feel happy.

Dad likes horse-riding on the beach but I'm not very keen on horse-riding. I'm scared of horses! Mum is bored with the beach. Today she's climbing in the mountains.

Lots of love

Tom

Mr and Mrs Smith

22 The Street

London

NW18 9TF

UK

11 **Listen and answer.**
3:31

12 **Listen and say.**
3:32

SOUNDS FUN!

The h**or**se is sn**or**kelling and the n**ur**se is s**ur**fing!

13 **Play the game.**

I'm horse-riding on the beach.

Horse-riding.

Talk about the pictures. Then listen and read.

  Act out the story.

Can understand a simple story / Can act out a story

16 What do you know?

17 Listen and read. Then answer the questions.
3:36

Save the Reefs!

You can find coral reefs in the sea in hot and sunny places. They are called the rainforests of the sea because a lot of fish and sea animals live on them. There are seahorses, sea snakes, starfish, butterfly fish, parrotfish and many more. There are a lot of pretty colours in the reef. How does this coral reef make you feel?

Now look at this coral reef. It's white and there are no fish or sea animals on it. The sea is too hot because of global warming and the coral reef is dead. How does this coral reef make you feel?

Please help us save the coral reefs.

1 Where can you find coral reefs?
2 Why are they called the rainforests of the sea?
3 Name three sea animals that live on a coral reef.
4 Why is the coral reef white?

18 Talk to your friend.

1 Which places are in danger in your country?
2 Which animals live there?

 PROJECT

Make a leaflet about protecting nature.

1 **Fold** a piece of paper in half.
2 **Draw** or stick photos inside and on the back of the leaflet.
3 **Write** a title and things we can do to protect nature.
4 **Share** your leaflet with the class.

19 **Listen and tick (✓).**

1 **a**  **b**    **2** **a**  **b**

3 **a**  **b**    **4** **a**  **b**

20 **Write in your notebook.**

1  What are you keen on?
I'm keen on ❓.

2  Are you keen on spiders?
No, I'm not.
I'm ❓.

3  Are you keen on sailing?
No, I'm bored ❓.

4  What are you terrified of?
❓ sharks.

21 **Choose a picture. Ask and answer.**

Are you keen on snorkelling?   Yes, I am.

I can identify some outdoor activities.
I can talk about doing outdoor activities.
I can understand a text about coral reefs.

Can assess what I have learnt in Unit 8

22 **Draw the chart in your notebook. Then write.**

HAVE FUN

Me	My friend	
Round 1		
Keen on	Terrified of	
1 _____	1 _____	☐
2 _____	2 _____	☐
3 _____	3 _____	☐
4 _____	4 _____	☐
Round 2		
Bored with	Scared of	
1 _____	1 _____	☐
2 _____	2 _____	☐
3 _____	3 _____	☐
4 _____	4 _____	☐

23 **Now play.**

Are you keen on surfing?

No, I'm not. My turn.

Now go to Poptropica English World

Lesson 8

Can use what I have learnt in Unit 8

Goodbye

1 🎧 3:38 **Listen and number.**

2 📖 **Read and match.**

1	Favolina Jolly	**a**	is keen on skateboarding.
2	Finley Keen	**b**	is very tired.
3	Sophie	**c**	is kayaking with Oliver.
4	Uncle James	**d**	is eating a banana next to a waterfall.
5	Coco	**e**	is keen on camping.

Can talk about what people are doing

Christmas

1 🎧 3:39 **Listen and read. Then answer the questions.**

turkey

sprouts

Christmas crackers

snowman

Hi! I'm Grace. This is me and my family on Christmas Day. We open our presents in the morning, then my mum cooks a special lunch. We eat turkey, potatoes, carrots and sprouts. Then we have Christmas pudding. Yum! We pull Christmas crackers. They go 'bang' and inside there are little presents, jokes and paper hats. What colour is my hat in the photo? In the afternoon I play with my presents. If it's snowy, I play snowball games with my brother or make a snowman in the garden.

1 When does Grace open her Christmas presents?

2 When do Grace and her family eat a special meal?

3 What do they eat?

4 What is Grace wearing in the photo?

5 Has Grace got any brothers or sisters?

2 3:40 / 3:41 **Listen and sing.**

My dad is hanging Christmas lights.
On Christmas Day, On Christmas Day.
My dad is hanging Christmas lights.
On Christmas Day in the morning.

My mum is cooking Christmas lunch...
My sister's playing snowball games...
And we are singing a Christmas song...

Mother's Day

1  **Listen and read.
Then answer the questions.**

rose

Mother's Day card

tea

toast

box of chocolates

Today is Sunday and it's Mother's Day. This is breakfast in bed for my mum. It's a treat because she makes breakfast for me and my dad every day. My mum likes toast and tea for breakfast. Today she's got a rose and some presents, too. My present for Mum is a box of chocolates!

1 Which day is Mother's Day?

2 Where is Mum having breakfast?

3 What is Mum having for breakfast?

4 What's in the box?

2 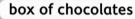 **Listen and sing.**

When I'm happy, when I'm sad,
You're always there.
When I'm good, when I'm bad,
You really care.

When I'm hungry, when I'm scared,
You know what to do.
So today's the day to say
A big THANK YOU!
Happy Mother's Day!

Can talk about Mother's Day

Name:

Name:

Name:

Name:

Name:

Name:

Name:

Name:

Name:

Name:

Name:

Name:

Name:

Name:

Name:

Name:

Name:

Name:

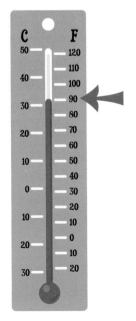

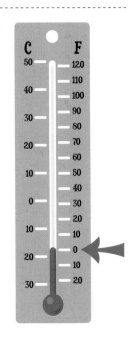

Name: _____

Name: _____

Name: _____

Name: _____

Name: _____

Name: _____

Name: _____

Name: _____

Name: _____

Name:

Name:

Name:

Name:

Name:

Name:

Name:

Name:

Name:

Name: _____

Name: _____

Name: _____

Name: _____

Name: _____

Name: _____

Name: _____

Name: _____

Name: _____

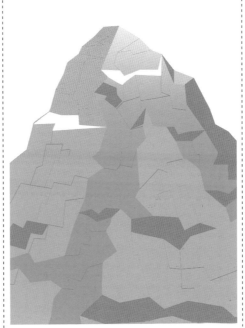
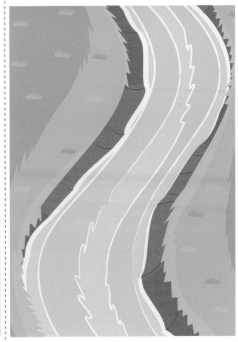

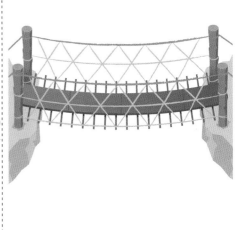

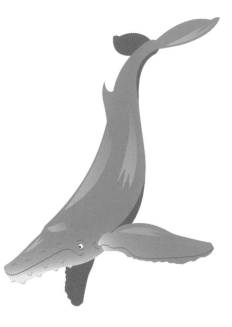

Name:

Name:

Name:

Name:

Name:

Name:

Name:

Name:

Name:

Name: _____

Name: _____

Name: _____

Name: _____

Name: _____

Name: _____

Name: _____

Name: _____

Name: _____

Name:

Name:

Name:

Name:

Name:

Name:

Name:

Name:

Name: